HOW  TO  S

GW01451361

# HOW TO START
# FLY FISHING

IAN WOOD

ERNEST BENN LIMITED · LONDON

*Published by Ernest Benn Limited*
*Bouverie House, Fleet Street, London, EC4A 2DL*

*First Impression 1966*
*Second Impression 1971*

© *Ernest Benn Limited 1971*

*Printed in Great Britain*

*ISBN 0 510-23601-4*

*Printed in Great Britain by photolitho-offset*
*by Cox & Wyman Limited, London, Fakenham and Reading*

# CONTENTS

# INTRODUCTION

IN MANY CASES an angler's life proceeds in a series of stages. To begin with he goes in for the simplest way of catching fish because at that stage his sole outlook is to deceive as many fish as possible at each outing, irrespective of the size or lack of cunning of such fish.

Later the angler may well find that he feels an urge to try something more difficult in the way of either fishing methods or fish. Gradually he finds that there can be immense satisfaction in catching fewer fish, but of better size, possibly through mastering a more difficult method of fishing which, when he started fishing, seemed beyond his skill.

Eventually, having tried out various methods among various fish, most enthusiasts settle down to one, or perhaps two methods and apply them to the pursuit of one or two kinds of fish.

You have of course, exceptions. There are those who are dedicated to coarse fishing with bait and who would not waste time going after trout or salmon. You have the trout or salmon fanatics who would not fish with bait for any fish and who have no interest in coarse fishing. Then there are the few who divide their time between coarse and game fishing.

For myself I am a trout and salmon addict and nowadays I fish only with the fly. That does not mean that I do not admire those who fish for other fish in other ways. Indeed I think that the coarse fisher of the English waters is worthy of the greatest admiration as a very sporting gentleman who goes to immense trouble and expends great skill to catch fish, all of which he returns to the water. What could be more sporting than that?

I am glad to think that in recent years more trout and even salmon men are following that coarse fishing lead and returning many more fish to the water than was the case in game fishing of the past.

*     *     *

In my boyhood days in Scotland the usual progress of a boy who wanted to fish followed a rather set pattern. He began by bait fishing in small streams or burns with the worm and only when these little waters were in flood. This gave him a chance of considerable reward for a minimum outlay of skill. Later he would try a bigger river with trout flies and eventually have a go at salmon fishing.

There was very little spinning in those days and the now popular fixed-spool reel was only beginning to make its appearance in rather crude form. Any spinning was done only for salmon with heavy tackle and free-running, centre-pin reels controlled by the thumb. Believe me, while you were learning to control one of those early spinning reels you also learned how to unravel the most appalling tangles of line! No wonder fly fishing was the easy way out then.

In my own case I caught my first trout on fly and it was at a later date that I enjoyed flood fishing with the worm. So with salmon—my first fish was on a fly and it was in later years that I learned spinning with the difficult centre-pin reel and then went on through almost all the spinning reels that were manufactured. Eventually I turned to the fly completely for the simple reason that I love fly fishing better than any other method I have tried.

As I have said, fly fishing in my young days was the easy way out. The intense pleasures I have had from it over the years make me forever glad that that was the position then. Today, as I see it, too many lads buy a fixed-spool reel, find it simple to work and then, gaining an impression that fly casting is difficult, they go on bait fishing or spinning even though they feel they would like to try the fly.

I am not going to say that there is anything wrong in this but I do feel that many of our younger anglers today would like to try fly fishing if only they had someone to guide them at the start. I know that this is the case because of many letters I receive in the course of editing the magazine *Trout and Salmon.*

It is therefore with that idea in mind that I write this little book. If in this way I can help even a few anglers to share the joy and the satisfaction that fly fishing has given to me over the years I will have been amply repaid.

CHAPTER I

# SELECTING A ROD

SOME EXPERIENCED ANGLERS will say that the beginner should buy the best rod he can for a start. I do not agree with this idea because the beginner has no experience of the various rod actions. Since the choice of a rod is a personal thing the beginner needs to have some experience of the use of a fly rod before he can decide what type is his personal choice.

With this in mind I think the beginner should start with a second-hand rod or, if he buys a new one he would be wise to keep to the cheaper range. I say this because after his first season he is almost sure to have formed his own opinion of rods for the job and is nearly certain to want to make a change.

If it is at all possible the novice should have the guidance of either an experienced angler or of a reputable tackle dealer when purchasing his first rod. Such help can be very valuable. On the other hand an enthusiastic beginner can find his own way remarkably well if the urge to fly fish is there. When I was a lad I had no help in making my fly fishing start yet I soon managed to catch some trout although I quickly formed new ideas about what my ideal rod should feel like.

In the old days one had a choice of either greenheart or split-cane rods and today there are glass rods and steel ones as well. I believe that in time to come the glass rod will possibly equal anything else the rod maker can produce. Meantime, however, I am old-fashioned enough to prefer the split-cane rod to any other and I strongly recommend that material to the beginner. He may well change to a rod of another material after he has had some experience—his personal choice may take him that way. He will not go far wrong if he starts with cane.

When the beginner first handles a few rods his choice might be of one with a whippy action. It is better though, to start with what might be termed a dry-fly action—that is a fairly stiff one. I think this will serve the learner-caster better that a soft-actioned rod.

What length should the rod be? The answer depends on what type of water the angler is likely to fish most often although any of the normal single-handed rod lengths will do so far as learning to cast goes. For small waters rods from say 7 ft. 6 in. to 8 ft. 6 in. should suit. Where bigger rivers are concerned 9 ft. or 9 ft. 6 in. might be chosen, while for really wide rivers and reservoir fishing another foot may be added to the length with advantage.

From the fish-catching point of view it is not wise to go to the very short rods that may be seen occasionally nowadays. In fact the beginner should err on the long side with his first rod because not all waters have grassy banks and where there are rushes or bushes along the banks the longer rod allows one to control a fish and perhaps to hold it out from such obstructions when necessary.

There are one or two things about rods that should be noted. Split-cane rods are amazingly strong and will stand up to years of very hard work. That is why, after you have had some experience and have come to know exactly what you like in the way of rod action, it can be a good thing to buy the best rod available.

There is, however, one governing condition—rods must have reasonable care taken of them. We all know for instance, that if you step on a rod it is likely to be broken. Even so we find anglers who persistently lay down their rods in the most careless way and simply ask for trouble. Never then, lay down your rod where there is a chance of it being trodden on by your own or another's foot. There is an old saying that it is bad luck to step over a rod. Whether you are superstitious or not always keep that saying in mind.

Believe me, it has proved to be bad luck on many occasions!

In the same way do not lay your rod against a rock or anything rough while you eat your lunch on a windy day. It can be badly scraped by treatment like that. Again this may seem obvious, but it is amazing how often one sees a fine rod so treated. Should you be much in boats keep the same thing in mind particularly if you are doing odd runs with an engine over rough water. When I fished Loch Lomond I had rubber-covered pieces of heavy wire set in holes in the gunwale and the rod was rested on one of those when not in use. Another thing I have seen is a rod tipping out over the side of a boat, never to be found again. So always be very careful how and where you lay down your rod be you ashore or afloat.

Often nowadays rods are carried, ready for fishing, in a car. Remember if you do this to wrap duster or handkerchief round the rod where it rests on probably, the window glass. If you are alone in the car gently close the window on the padding so that the rod does not flap about. Should you have a companion let him hold the rod in his hand where it goes out through the window. If by chance you are carrying two rods in this way it is a good plan to tie another duster round the top parts of the rods to stop their flapping about and tangling the two lines.

Never leave a rod resting against a wall overnight so that it has a bend in it. If the rod is to be left up it should be laid on suitable supports on a wall or laid flat on a shelf out of danger's way. In most cases indeed, it is wise policy to dismantle your rod every night and so save any risk of damage.

Damp is a rod's great enemy. If you have fished through a wet day always dry your rod before you put it in its case. Even after that when you arrive home take the rod from its case again and place it in an airy room so that all traces of damp disappear from it and its case.

There are various types of ferrules fitted to rods these days but I prefer the straightforward, suction joints. These are very reliable and with a little care will be trouble-free over the years. Ferrule stoppers are often mislaid or lost and it is a good thing to attach them in some way to the rod case. If you do lose them it is worth while renewing them because they not only keep the dirt out of the female ferrule but protect it from damage.

These ferrules are very accurately made and on no account should they be touched with emery or sand paper. If the fitting is too tight clean both the male and the female side with a dry, soft rag and rub the male ferrule with a soft (4B) pencil. If after long wear the fitting becomes slightly loose a temporary cure can be found by rubbing the male end with a piece of ordinary wax candle. I have known this to keep a slack-fitting ferrule gripping well for a whole season with only the occasional application of the wax. Eventually of course, a new ferrule must be fitted.

Should a ferrule, that normally slides in a good fit, feel stiff to put together, do not force it. Clean both sides with a soft rag and use the trick of rubbing the male end in the hair at the nape of your neck. The slight oiliness so spread over the ferrule will make it slide home in the normal way. But clean and treat it as above at the first opportunity.

If by chance the ferrule sticks when you come to dismantle a rod be sure that when you begin to us some force on it you grip the metal and not the cane. If you try force through the medium of the cane you will probably damage the rod. Should you need the assistance of a friend be sure that he too grips the ferrule and not the cane. As a last resort with a stuck ferrule you can try heating the metal with the flame from a match or a petrol lighter. This expands the female side and should then allow the male to be withdrawn.

Always keep an eye on the top and bottom rings of your rod as probably they will be agate-type lined. If one of these linings happens to crack it can very soon damage a good fly line. To renew a ring is not a difficult job so long as you can make a neat whipping. First of all you fix the

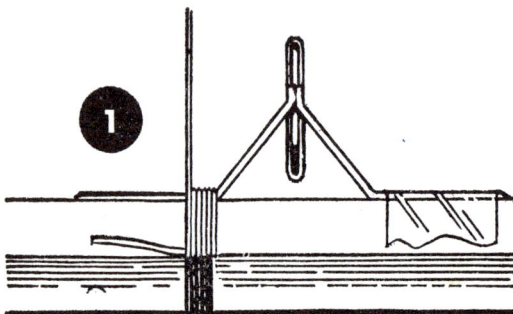

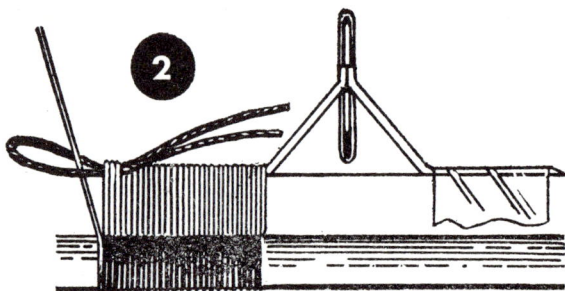

*Whipping a ring*

new ring in its correct place by holding one end with a spring-type clothes peg or any other type of clip that will go over it and the rod; a rubber band can be used for this as can adhesive tape. You can if you wish set the ring legs in an adhesive as well. Then start binding with a suitable silk thread from the inside end of the ring leg. The easiest way to finish the binding is to place a loop of the thread you are using along the binding when you come to the last three turns. Bind over this loop and when you have finished binding put the end of your thread through the loop and then smartly pull the ends of the loop back so that the end of the thread is pulled underneath the last three bindings. When the whipping has been done over both legs of the ring a first-quality varnish should then be used over the whippings and a second coat applied after the first one has dried. Varnish should be worked into any little holes or hollows between whippings and rod.

Give your rod some care and attention and it will last you for a very long time. Many anglers strip and varnish their own rods when necessary and if you like doing that sort of thing there is no reason why you should not do so. For myself I feel that a good rod is worthy of an occasional visit to the makers for a complete check-up and overhaul. The highly-skilled professional hands can always be trusted to do a first-class job and the rod will come back to you as good as new.

## CHAPTER II

# REELS, LINES AND BACKING

IN THE OLD DAYS when rods and reels were both much heavier than they are today there was much talk about selecting a reel that would balance your rod. Nowadays, however, when rods and reels are so much lighter there are indeed few reels, suitable for the angling purpose in mind, that would balance a rod. Because of this very lightness you need not worry too much about balance unless you are either a perfectionist or have a weak casting wrist.

The main thing is to select a reel suitable for the fishing you intend to do. There are any number of makes of reels on the market today so that there should be no difficulty in finding one to suit your purpose and your pocket.

If you are likely to be fishing a small stream where the fish do not run large you could be quite happy with one of the lightweight reels. Beware of this, however, if you are likely to have the occasional day on a big river or on a reservoir where fish may run large.

The trouble with many small, neat reels is that they have very narrow drums, the idea being that they can give a quick rate of recovery when wound in. However, it must be remembered that a fast recovery also means a fast run out. Further, the modern plastic lines which are so popular are much bulkier than the older, oil-dressed, silk lines. If therefore, you run a floating plastic line on to a small reel you will find that the line will probably fill the reel leaving no space for backing line. It takes little imagination to picture what might happen if, with no backing, you hooked a large fish that ran off wildly as many big fish do. You might indeed, lose the fish of a lifetime.

I suggest therefore, that unless you are absolutely tied to

small streams you should always have a reel that is capable of taking a good length of backing. It is seldom perhaps, that the backing will be called into service but it is for ever a comfort to know that it is there when needed. I would say that when picking a reel it is wise to err on the big side rather than on the small side.

There are many today who like a reel which is operated with the left hand. This, say the enthusiasts, means that when a fish is hooked you do not have to change over hands to play it. That is quite true but in all my fishing I have had right-hand winding fly reels and I can never recall having changed over hands when a fish has been hooked. No doubt I must have changed over but the movement was so automatic that it went unnoticed.

For years I did much loch fishing for salmon from boats. Often I fished with my reel upwards so as to save the rod from taking a slight set. There again I can never recall letting the rod turn in my hands after a fish was hooked although of course, that movement must have taken place at every hooking.

However, while I may prefer right-hand reels for my fly fishing that is not to say that you will be wrong to pick a left-hand wind if you so fancy. There are indeed, reels on the market today which can be changed over from right to left in a matter of seconds.

The drag or check action of all the better reels is adjustable. This is a very useful feature because nothing is more annoying than to have to work with a drag that is too heavy or too light all the time. I always use adjustable-check reels and fish with the check set just stronly enough to stop line from running out from the force of casting or shooting line. After a fish is hooked more tension can be put on if the strength of the fish warrants it.

There are reels on the market which have no winding handle at all. They are spring loaded and when a fish pulls stronger than the spring the line runs out. Similarly when the pull of the fish is less than that of the spring the line is automatically recovered by the reel. I have not used such a reel so I cannot say anything for or against it. I am sure however, that a beginner should avoid it because through his first efforts with orthodox reels he will soon learn to have "hands" in the same way as do horse riders or pianists. He will learn to feel and to judge the strength of his fish and will soon be able to judge just how much pressure he may safely put on any fish he is playing. Later these automatic reels might be all right but to begin with—no.

Reels are like rods. They will stand up to long and hard use so long as they are given some attention. The internal parts must always be kept clean and oiled or coated with a light grease. Never let sand or grit find a way on to the mechanism of a reel. If such foreign matter does get in you will probably be aware of its presence from the rough sound. Even if you only suspect that dirt has gained an entry waste no time in giving the reel a thorough cleaning and, of course, before you assemble it again be sure that it is thoroughly lubricated.

So far as lines are concerned anglers in these days are well supplied. There are lines made from various materials some of which sink rapidly, sink normally or float on the surface. Many anglers use a floating line for all their trout fishing whether they are using dry fly or wet. The main reason for this is that a floating line can be controlled more easily and more efficiently than a sunk one.

With the great variation of lines and of their component materials there is also variation in the weights of lines. Since the weight of a line is important when one comes to select one for a particular rod the newcomer to fishing might find himself in something of a quandary were he left to select a line by himself. It so happens, however, that the manufacturers of fishing tackle saw this difficulty arising as new materials were used for line making and after much thought they evolved a standard of line specification.

The result is that now the tackle dealer can advise the angler what lines will suit his particular rod. In fact some rod manufacturers now mark their rods with the line specification these rods require. Others give the specification in their catalogues. The beginner therefore would be well advised to consult a good dealer when it comes to buying a fly line.

The beginner will have to decide what type of line he will require. For all general trout, fly-fishing purposes I suggest that one of the good makes of double-tapered floating line would prove the best buy for the novice. Such lines are fattest in the middle of their thirty-yard length and they taper towards each end. If necessary, after some use, a line of this type can be reversed on the reel. Another advantage is that in most makes the last yard or so tends to go under the surface of the water thus being ideal for wet-fly fishing.

Earlier I wrote about the importance of having as much backing on the reel as possible. Backing is usually of un-dressed material such as silk or flax; it may be of plaited nylon but not of nylon monofilament. For various reasons monofil is not advisable behind the casting line.

You want your reel, when complete with line and back-ing, to be fairly full, but be sure it is not so full that if you have to wind in very quickly when playing a fish the line builds up and fouls the frame of the reel. So leave a little space with this in mind.

The beginner always wonders how to judge the correct amount of backing to put on a reel so that when the line is attached the reel will be nicely full. A very simple way to arrive at a solution is to begin by winding the casting line on first. Then add the backing, winding on sufficient to fill the reel as required. Next you run off the whole of the back-ing and the line and refill the reel starting with the backing first. This simple reversal method can save much trial-and-error work.

Again, I have seen all sorts of joints made by beginners between line and backing. I have even seen an ordinary knot used—a knot that would not have gone through the rings of the rod. In such a case the angler would have been

19

as well off without any backing at all.

I consider the joining of line to backing an important thing because if it is not well done it is possible to lose a good fish with all your casting line. I am going to give you therefore two ways of joining line and backing. Both of these descriptions have appeared in the magazine—*Trout and Salmon.*

The first of the methods is the old and well-tried splicing of the two lines. The following description was written by R. Barraud:

1. Scrape off the dressing from an inch of the line.
2. Fray out a quarter-of-an-inch of both line and backing.
3. Flatten off toward the frayed ends by beating.
4. Wax the ends thoroughly with cobbler's wax.
5. Wax a length of tying silk and tie line and backing together at "A" half-an-inch from extreme ends.
6. With silk end "A-B" bind line and backing tightly together and be careful they do not get twisted in the process—they must lie parallel. Continue just beyond the frayed end on to the single line.
7. Bind back again to point "A"; twist together a few times both silks "A-B" and "A-C" and bind from "A" to end of other frayed end. At that point cut off closely the silk end "A-C" and continue beyond the frayed end with silk "A-B" only. Finish with a neat whipping of about four turns.
8. Wax over the whole job well, then roll the splice between two hard smooth surfaces to a nice even torpedo shape. Most instructions tell you to varnish over the wax. But the varnish will not only become hard and brittle it will only be a thin skin anyway and do no good at all. To keep the joint pliable and slippery just rub it with a bit of wax candle now and again.

The second method is one that has been increasingly used over the last few years. I have tried it and found it a very satisfactory way of joining the two lines. That well-known American angler and writer, Joe Brooks calls this the

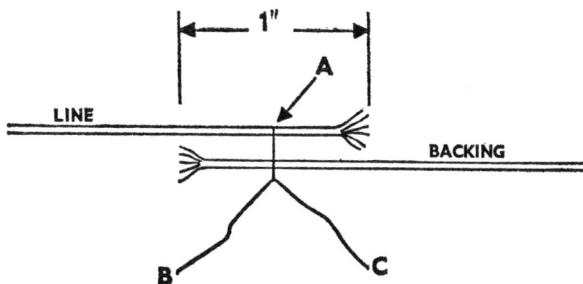

*Splicing line to backing*

Nail knot but it is known here as the Needle knot. It can be tied with the help of a tapered nail, a needle or a piece of small gauge tube. It can even be tied with a piece of hollow grass or rush. The following description is taken from an article on the Needle knot that was written by John Turner:

First you get a needle with an eye big enough to let the backing pass through easily. I suggest a tapestry needle as it has a blunt point, but a darning needle would do. (Tapestry needles are cheap; a packet of five or so can be had for a few coppers).

Lay the fly line, the needle and the backing together, holding them between the finger and thumb of one hand. With the other hand wind the point of the backing round the fly line, the needle and itself for half-a-dozen turns. Then pass the point through the eye of the needle.

Holding the coils between the finger and thumb pull the needle free from the coils.

Pull gently on the backing point and on the other part of the backing alternately till the coils close together neatly and then pull firmly on both together till the knot bites into the fly line.

When I use the Needle knot for joining line to back-

21

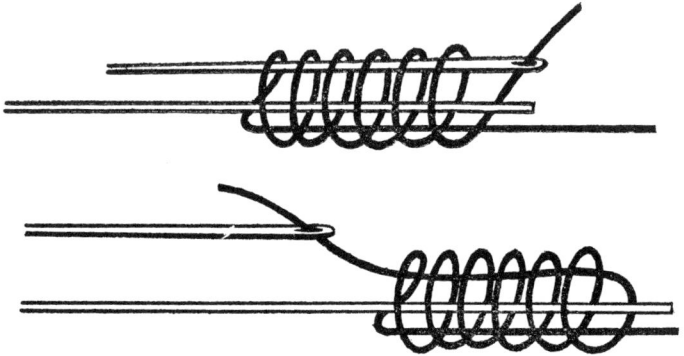

*Needle knot*

ing I always whip it over the same way as I would a splice. This is to make sure that the knot slips through the rings smoothly.

Now you are complete with rod, line and reel. Buy yourself a spool of nylon about 4½ lb. or 5 lb. breaking strain and you are ready to begin learning to cast.

Just one final word about the reel that is now full of line. Never wind the end of the line on to the drum. It can find its way under the line coils on the drum and this may be found out only when you are playing a fish and the reel jams. So always either leave a foot or eighteen inches of line hanging from the reel or else lightly knot the end of the line round one of the convenient parts of the reel frame.

## CHAPTER III

# STARTING TO CAST

CASTING A FLY frightens many beginners before they even try it. Right away let me say that there is nothing very difficult about it, the main point to keep in mind for a start is that rhythm is the thing. There is no need for jerky movement, nor do you need to use force; try to make the rod do the work for you—that is what it is there for.

Probably you will want to make a start on your lawn or on some such open space. If so, put up your rod and attach the reel, thread the line through the rings and then attach about six feet of nylon to the end of the line. If you turn to pages 26/29 you will see how to tie the knots necessary for this. Then, to the end of the nylon attach a small piece of rag—perhaps a piece about an inch square and rolled up. This piece of rag will give you a weight about that of a fly at the end of the nylon, but it will not hook you or anyone else if you make a bad cast.

Go out to your selected open space and pull off line from the reel so that you have about three times the length of the rod lying on the grass. Pick up the rod and holding it approximately parallel to the ground walk slowly backwards until the line is lying straight ahead of the rod and of you. Now imagine you are standing in front of a clock face and assuming an easy stance, lift the rod until it is about 10 on the clock face. From there try to lift the line cleanly off the grass by raising the rod smartly from the 10 o'clock position, accelerating the lift about 11 o'clock and stopping the rod's movement smartly between 12 and 1. The line should have lifted well out behind you and when you stopped the rod, fallen down reasonably straight on the grass.

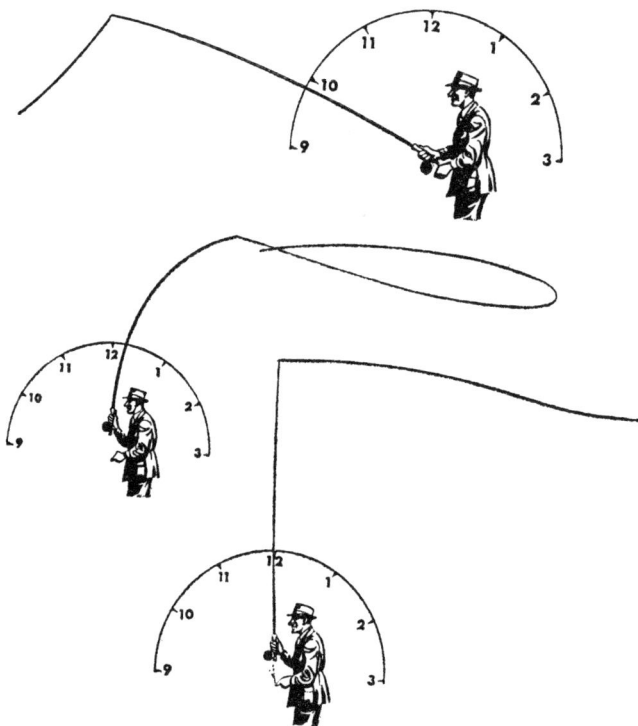

*Starting to cast*

If the line has fallen badly walk forward slowly until it has straightened out. Then, from not further behind you then between 1 and 2 on the clock, bring the rod smartly forward stopping it at 10. The line should have come forward and should lie in front of you on the grass.

Try this kind of single action cast a few times before you try a complete cast. Start your complete cast effort with the line on the grass in front of you as when you first began, lift it smartly and stop the rod between 12 and 1. This time pause there only long enough to let the line straighten out in the air (but not long enough to let it fall). When you judge it has straightened out behind you start the forward drive, stopping the rod at 10 as before. If the line falls reasonably straight on the grass in front of you, you have successfully completed your first cast.

Keep on practising until you are satisfied that you have found the right timing for the back pause. Always remember that the backwards drive must throw the line upwards and that at the end of the forward drive you should aim at a point about three feet above the grass (later of course, the water) with your fly. Never cast it down at the water; if you do that you will make a heavy, splashy cast whereas if you aim above the surface the fly will then fall gently down.

As you become more proficient you can introduce a slight outwards movement of the rod as you lift on the back cast and then a very slight inwards movement as you come forward. This will help you to avoid hitting your rod with the fly on the forward stroke—a fault that often worries beginners and which, apart from spoiling a cast, can lead to broken hook points.

After you have mastered the straightforward cast with a short line you should try to shoot some line. Shooting line enables you to cast a longer line than you can pick up from the water. When using the shooting technique therefore, you must handline in the extra line you shot before making your next cast.

To try shooting, stop your ordinary casting when the line is lying on the grass in front of you. Keep the rod at 10 o'clock and with the left hand pull from the reel some two yards of line. Let this line hang down from the reel and hold the line with your left hand to stop it running up the rings. Cast in the normal way but when the forward thrust is made let go the line from the left hand. The weight of the casting line and its forward movement should pull the extra two yards out through the rings. Before you cast again pull in the two extra yards with the left hand running the line under the index finger of the right hand as you pull in. By using the finger of the right hand thus you can check the line between the pulls from the left hand.

When you become proficient in shooting—and only practice will teach you the exact timing of the shoot—you will be able to shoot much more than two yards. However, two yards is sufficient extra line for the beginner to try.

Having reasonably mastered normal casting the only thing you must try before going to the water is false casting. False casting is a method of letting out line used often when dry-fly fishing but frequently useful in any type of fly fishing. To false cast you can start off with a line only the length of your rod. Flick that line back smartly and as you do so pull from the reel with the left hand two or three feet of line. As your flick cast is brought forward let that left-hand line go. It will shoot out thereby lengthening your

*Blood Bight knot*

26

casting line. Keep your line in the air by casting back and forward and at each cast add more line from the reel until you have the length that you require.

Having become reasonably proficient at casting you will now want to make a start on the river, but before you do that you will have to learn how to make a nylon cast and tie on a fly. All you have to do is to learn a few knots, and here they are. First, the way to make a loop for the line end of your nylon. This is known as the Blood Bight knot. Then to join the cast loop to your casting line you can use an ordinary Figure-of-Eight knot.

*Half Blood knot*

To tie a fly to the end of your cast you can use either the Half Blood knot or the single or double Turle knot. To begin with you should have only one fly at the end of your cast but later you may want to attach more than one. To do this you must have dropper pieces of nylon to which to attach flies other than that one at the end. You may make droppers by using the Treble Overhand.

For wet-fly or nymph fishing you can use a cast of level nylon but when you come to use dry fly it is better to grade your cast. For wet fly a cast about two feet less than the length of your rod should do. For dry fly you can grade your cast something like—2½ ft. of 6 lb. breaking strain, 3 ft. of 5 lb. breaking strain with finally a point of 2½/3 ft.

27

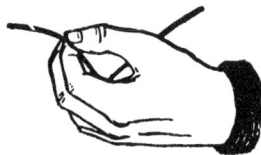

*Figure-of-eight line recovery*

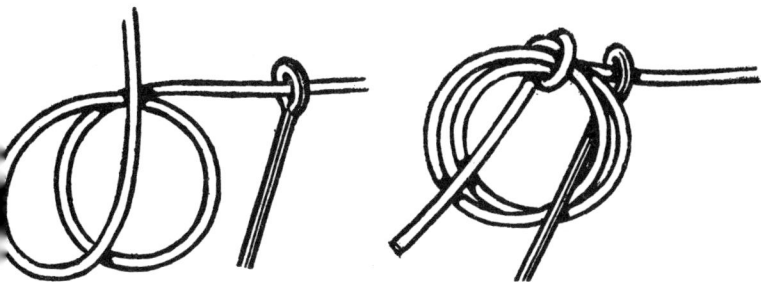

*Double Turle knot*

*Treble Overhand knot*

of 4 lb. breaking strain. Later you may want to grade your cast over a much wider range, but this grading will do for a start.

There are incidentally, different ways of gripping a rod but for all single-handed casting I think it is best always to grip with the thumb lying upwards along the cork. In this way you have complete control of the rod and a normally firm grip is all that is necessary. There is no need to grip tightly.

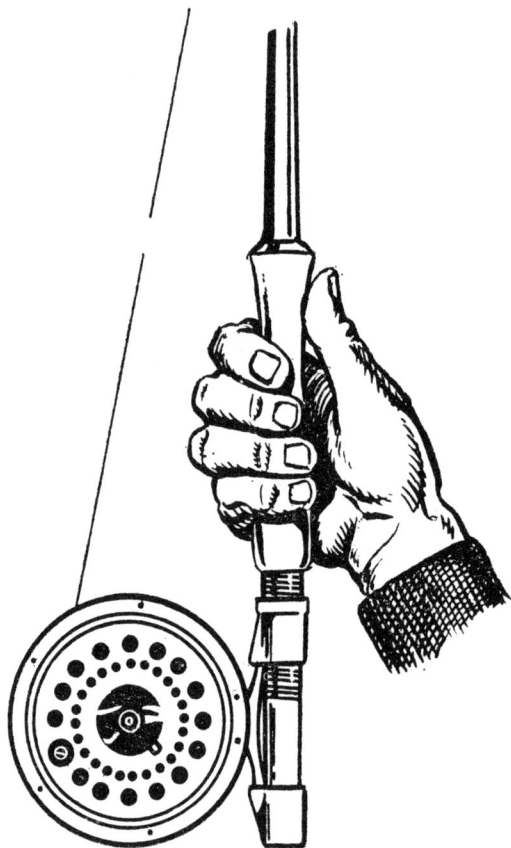

*Gripping the rod*

# CHAPTER IV

# STARTING WITH WET FLY

WHEN YOU GO DOWN to the river for the first time there is one important thing you must note, and that does not concern casting. It concerns your approach to the water.

Too often you seen anglers going right to the side of the water and then beginning to put up their rods. This you should never do. Always prepare your tackle back from the water and when finally you approach to begin to fish take care to do so quietly and cautiously. The blundering, noisy approach is not good fishing and is sure to make your catch light.

When walking by the water always keep well back from the bank. Even on a big river this is good policy. Any fish you disturb go racing away and their hurried movement is noted by other fish that may not have seen you. And so the alarm is spread.

In good fishing then, your approach must always be quiet, and any movement you make when fish might see you should be slow and cautious. If there are stones by the river never walk on them carelessly for vibrations travel into the water and alert the fish. Keep this in mind too, when you go fishing from a boat. Always in fishing study to be quiet.

By the river make use of every scrap of cover. That does not mean that you must always be behind a bush or long grass. You can make use of cover often by standing in front of it. The basic idea of cover indeed, is in making use of it to keep your outline from being silhouetted against the sky. Where the banks are bare you may get on better if you kneel to cast instead of standing and if you can cast from a bank where you have the sun in front of you rather than from one where the sun is behind you, then do so. Shadows are very frightening to fish and when the sun is at your back, especially in the evening, the shadow of both your body and your rod can scare fish many yards from where you are standing.

You will almost always wear wading boots when you go to fish. Even so, wade as little as possible and try not to wade at all unless it is absolutely necessary. This is import-ant on small waters and especially if the pool you are fishing is still. The ripples you send out are first-class warning signals. This applies too, to loch or reservoir fishing.

If you must wade do so as slowly and as quietly as possible, and do remember that the fish are not always lying on the far side of the river. We all seem to get that impression and try to reach the far bank with our flies. A moment's thought, however, will show that we would do the same thing if we were on the other bank!

The same applies to loch fishing. When we fish from the bank we try to cast as far out as possible, yet when we go in a boat on the same water we try to keep inshore and cast into the shallows as much as possible.

Bear these things in mind. Always go quietly. Wade as little as possible. Make use of any cover and do not keep straining yourself to cast a long line. There may be a good fish almost under your rod point if your approach has been careful and he will be easier to hook on a short line than on a long one.

So much for approach. You put up your tackle then, well back from the water and on this occasion you are going to fish with a single wet fly at the end of your nylon. About six feet of nylon will be long enough for you at this stage.

Perhaps the river has lengths of tree-lined banks with the occasional open bit here and there. Later you will think nothing of going to a wooded bit and flicking your fly neatly under the branches. Meantime, pick an open bit.

Keep well back from the water and go upstream past the top of the pool you mean to try; go past the top of it even if that should mean going into the trees. There, out of sight of the water you are to fish slide down the steep bank and prepare to creep down to the neck of your pool.

Before you start, however, see that you have wet your fly and cast so that they do not float. Dabble them in the water and if there is any fine mud about rub some down the nylon. Then quietly approach your selected place.

Start casting with quite a short line, lengthening it only after you are sure you have covered all the water possible. Cast out almost straight across the stream and let your fly swing round with the current. Do not hurry your fishing. A slow fly is often better than one worked fast. Try to let it sink a bit now and then—in other words vary your tactics and after you have covered the water from your first stance, take a cautious step downstream and begin to repeat the procedure.

Trout often lie beside rocks, boulders, tree stumps or tree roots that are in the water. If you see anything like these in your pool be sure to try your fly around them before you move on.

The rough water at the heads of pools is always a good place to try especially in warm weather. Where the rough water extends across the whole width of the river the fishing is straightforward. But where, as you so often find, there is a rush of water about midstream with slack eddies on each side of it, you must manipulate your line so as to avoid the flies being dragged. This line control is called mending the line. It is done by a circular motion of the wrist which makes the rod point move in the same way so that you can throw a roll of line—travelling from the rod point towards the fly—either upstream or downstream as required. This mending motion can be learned easily with a little practice.

If, for instance, you cast your fly into the rough water in midstream and your line lies across some slack water between that rough water and your rod point you should mend in a downstream direction so that your line tends to keep pace with the fly in the rough. If you do not do this the fly will be dragged by the line and will simply be whipped out of the rough before any fish has had time to take it. If by chance you want to put your fly in slack water on the far side of the rough then you must mend your line in an upstream curve, perhaps several times, to keep it from rushing ahead of the fly and dragging the fly with it.

When a trout takes your fly in downstream fishing you will perhaps not see it but you will feel the pluck of it. At that instant you should tighten with a very short wrist movement. Many people refer to this hooking movement as 'striking' but I always feel that 'striking' gives the beginner the wrong idea of the movement. If one really strikes hard there is every chance that the nylon will be broken whereas if a short but smart tightening movement from the wrist is made the hook should be set and the nylon in no danger of breaking. Never tighten violently. Always strive to control the movement so that there is nothing rough about it.

Again, when you hook a fish do not be rough with it. You may be firm in your playing of it but the firmness must be governed by a sympathetic hand. Always keep the rod up so that the bend of it absorbs the strain between the fish and you. If you make a point of keeping the rod bent you should not suffer any breakage. On the other hand if you point the rod at the fish you cancel out the shock-absorbing qualities of the rod and put all the strain on cast and line. Then you may well find that the cast will not stand the strain. After all, should you catch your fly on a high branch so that there is nothing for it but to break, the procedure you adopt is to point the rod at the fly and pull on the line. Incidentally if you have to do that always look away from the direction of the fly at the moment of breaking. Occasionally the fly comes away and it can, if the line is long enough, speed back and hit you. By turning your face away you at least save your eyes from danger.

When you have played your fish your next job is to net it and with a fish of ordinary proportions this should provide no difficulty. Always place your net in the water and bring your fish over it. Then lift the net and go well back from the water before you take it from the meshes. If you intend to keep the fish be sure to kill it immediately. A smart tap on the back of the head will do the job cleanly and quickly.

In the case of small fish which you do not wish to retain there is no need to handle them at all. Indeed, you do not need to net them. Simply shorten your line until you can grip' the cast a few inches above the hook and then slide your finger and thumb down the nylon until you have a firm grip of the hook shank. Hold the fish close to the surface of of the water and then give a sharp shake with the finger and thumb holding the hook. The fish should drop off. Even when a fish is badly hooked and may require a second shake to free it much less damage will be done to it in this way than by handling it to remove the hook.

I said there should be no difficulty in netting a fish of ordinary proportions, but there might be panic in the mind of a beginner if he finds he has hooked a fish much bigger than he expected. He will almost certainly begin to wonder how he can land it. Even if the fish is bigger than the diameter of your landing net you will be able to net it, but do not try to scoop it into the net either head or tail first. The golden rule here is to make up your mind to net the middle cut of the fish and forget the other bits of it. In other words you must manoeuvre the fish right across the net. If you lift the net before the head of the fish is far enough past the net ring the fish will simply slide out of the net. On the other hand if you take the head right over (and try to net that middle cut) you will find that the fish folds upwards nicely and slips into the meshes.

Maybe one day you will find that you have hooked a fish much too big to go into your net or that you have left your net at home. In such circumstances there is no need to be unduly worried. You can beach your fish. The term 'beach' does not mean that you have to find an actual beach to carry out this method of bringing your fish ashore. Certainly if you can find a gently sloping piece of sand or fine gravel so much the better, but on many waters there are no such places. On every water, however, there are many little inlets—the kind of places that a small boy might use to harbour his toy boat, and such tiny inlets are capable of taking a played-out fish. Beaching is a favourite method of landing procedure for salmon. Even with these big fish only a small inlet is needed to bring them safely within reach. I remember once beaching a salmon on a mass of trailing willow branches—a risky procedure perhaps, but it worked.

When you have a fish you want to beach you must play it until it is completely under control. Then, keeping your rod up and with a reasonably short line, walk slowly backwards guiding the fish towards the beaching place you have selected. The pressure you are applying, combined with the flapping of the fish, will slide it out of the water.

After you have fished downstream a few times you should try casting upstream. This, particularly in smaller waters, is a better approach. The main idea behind upstream casting is that since fish lie facing the current they are easier to approach from behind. Upstream fishing can be very effective with a wet fly and later when you fish dry fly you will find that upstream casting is essential in most circumstances.

Fishing upstream is more difficult than fishing down. In downstream work the current straightens out your line at each cast and swings your fly round for you. In upstream work, after you cast up or up and across you have to recover line with your left hand as the current drifts the fly back towards you. Do not pull on the fly when you do this—hand line at a rate which will just keep you in touch with the fly without acting on the fly itself.

As I have said earlier your approach to the water is probably the most important thing in your fishing. You cannot expect a shy fish like the trout to ignore either you or your shadow and go on feeding. If you scare your fish for a start the best of tackle and the finest casting will not be of any use thereafter. So do bear that in mind at all times. Make use of every scrap of cover, move quietly and slowly and for ever try to fit in with the surroundings. If you act thus you are well on the way to becoming a good angler.

*     *     *

What kind of creature is this trout that you are going to try to catch? To begin with, the most important point to remember is that the trout is a shy and easily disturbed fish. It will not tolerate noise, vibration or a clumsy approach to the water.

During the daytime the bigger trout, which, of course, are the fish you are trying to catch, are probably lying out in midstream. The smaller fellows may well be feeding or playing about in the side shallows and although you are after the big fish you must not ignore the little ones.

If you make a clumsy approach to the river's edge you will scare the little fish which will then dash wildly for the deeper water. Now, a trout of any size dashing away from anything in fear is an immediate warning to any fish that sees it. In other words you set an alarm bell ringing through the pool.

You cannot approach a pool without disturbing the little fish along the water's edge, but the slower and quieter your approach the less the disturbed fish will dash off. This may be repeating what I have already written, but it will emphasize the importance of approach.

I have said that during the day the bigger fish are likely to be in midstream. They do not always lie there, however, and at times even during the day you may find some of them close in by the bank so long as there is a fair depth of water. In the evening or the early morning you may find the better fish far in the shallows. The less bright the daylight the more fish seem to gain courage and leave the deeps and their comparative safety for the good feeding in the shallows.

When waters are low and the weather warm the places to look for your fish are in the rougher runs where the water is likely to give more oxygen than in the stiller stretches. Sometimes they will lie in what we might think are rough currents that must take much energy from any fish simply to hold its position. Where fish are found in very rough water you may be sure that they are taking advantage of some underwater shelter however small that shelter may be. I have heard it said for instance, that trout never lie behind boulders in the way many writers seem to suggest that they do. Trout do lie behind boulders because I have watched them in just such positions. Often they lie with their heads pointing downstream, because the water, curling round the boulder forms a backlash which in fact flows in an upstream direction although it might not appear thus to the casual human observer.

Good trout often lie in little pools that have tree roots forming a tangle at the side. Places like that are always worth a cast or two but the angler should be ready to hold any fish he may hook firmly from the start. A trout lying in such a place is sure to make for the shelter of the roots the moment he is hooked.

The one great point one should keep in mind about the trout is that it is almost always ready to eat anything that comes within its reach and looks edible. True, there may be short spells when the fish may lose interest in passing food morsels but in the main they are always ready to pick up what they can. I have often thought that fish spend their time much in the same way as do the birds. We know that the birds spend almost all their time picking here and there with only short spells when they stop feeding to preen themselves or to have a bath. Their main object in life is in the search for food. So with the trout and if we keep this in

38

mind it will help to keep our enthusiasm going when the fishing seems to be poor.

In fishing only one thing is certain. If you do not keep your flies in the water you will not catch fish.

## CHAPTER V

# STARTING WITH DRY FLY

A FTER YOU HAVE mastered wet-fly fishing there is little doubt that you will have the urge to try dry or floating fly. You may even have an opportunity to have a cast on one of the famous southern chalk streams where dry-fly fishing was born. To use a dry fly is a most delightful way of fishing. It is not particularly difficult, but you must be accurate in your casting and again particularly careful in your approach to your fish.

Generally for dry-fly work a slightly stiffer rod is used so that the fly may be cast cleanly and neatly. However, the rod you have can be made to perform in a satisfactory way so long as when you cast you do so well above the surface of the water so that the fly falls lightly and so that there is no line splash. You may get away with clumsy casting when fishing wet fly but you will not get away with it in dry-fly work for the fish you are after have their eyes on the surface and any splashing will at once put them down. So long as you are prepared to proceed with great care and to cast neatly you need not fear that dry-fly fishing is going to be too difficult for you.

In chalk-stream fishing many anglers cast only after they have seen a fish rise and do not, as a rule, fish the water as one does in wet-fly fishing. There is no reason why you should not fish the water, especially in northern streams, should you so wish although it is more rewarding to cast to a specific fish and to hook it than to take it otherwise.

With dry fly you fish upstream or upstream and across almost all the time. On occasion you may be able to reach a fish lying in a difficult place by floating the fly downstream, but such occasions are few and far between on the average water.

You must try to avoid drag on your fly at all times. There are times, it must be agreed, when a fish will take a fly that is dragging but, in the main, drag on a fly will put an interested fish off.

If you decide to have a go at dry fly a good plan is to make a number of casts on a river that has a fair current flowing through it. Do not worry about trying to catch fish, but simply cast and then watch your fly and your line. You will soon learn what the various current drags can do and you will save yourself much frustration when you go out after trout.

When you have a good idea of the difficulties you have to contend with in drag and how to overcome them so that the fly floats down naturally, you are ready to try for a fish. To begin with you should wait until you see a trout rising to a natural fly and then try to deceive it with your artificial. Approach to within casting distance with the greatest of caution, then, letting out line through a series of false casts until you judge you can reach the rise area, you make your cast. Try to land your fly about, or upstream of, the head of the fish you saw rising.

As the fly drifts down towards you, you must take up the slack line keeping in touch with the fly but avoiding any tendency to pull on it. If nothing happens repeat the cast.

Sometimes your fish will rise beautifully and take your fly with no trouble. At other times the fish will turn downstream and follow the fly for a bit before taking it, and at other times it will ignore all your efforts. If it does ignore your fly do not worry too much about it or blame yourself entirely because even the most experienced anglers find this sort of thing happening to them from time to time. Only if this goes on must you try to find out if you are doing anything wrong. The best way to find out that is to ask an experienced fisher to watch your efforts and suggest where you may be going wrong.

When a trout rises to your floating fly you must resist the urge to tighten immediately. There may be times when a fish takes with a splutter and hooks itself, but the normal rise to a floating fly is rather a slow business and indeed you may see the fish break the surface before it has touched the fly. The best thing to do is to steel yourself not to tighten at all. You still will tighten of course, but that little delay may make all the difference to the result.

For fishing dry fly your nylon should be carefully graded so that it rolls out nicely when cast. Your end piece should be about three-pound breaking strain. Light nylon at the fly is necessary otherwise the fly—especially if you are fishing with very small floaters—will tend to be pulled under the surface. While the preparations that are sold for making dry flies float are quite efficient when applied by the waterside it is a good thing to treat the flies you may use the night before. When treated at home and allowed to dry thoroughly they seem to float for a long period. When you do treat them after you have caught a fish or when they have become waterlogged you should false cast a few times to flick off any surplus flotant and to dry the fly as much as possible before fishing it again.

There is, of course, the substance called amadou which was at one time used widely for the drying of sodden flies. Nowadays the real material is rather scarce although there are substitutes to be had. For myself I find that a clean, absorbent duster in which to squeeze the fly does just about as well. Thereafter a few false casts and finally a blow or two of exhaled breath will make the fly ready for treatment with flotant.

## CHAPTER VI

# STILL-WATER FLY FISHING

O WING TO THE FORMATION of new reservoirs throughout the country still-water fishing for trout has become increasingly popular over the last few years. The river fisher who goes for the first time to fish a lake or reservoir usually finds his main difficulty is to guess where the trout may be. In a river he knows the various spots where he may expect a fish to rise but when faced with a wide expanse of water with no features about it he is inclined to feel somewhat lost.

Trout in still water cruise about in their search for food. Sometimes they patrol the deep water while at other times they haunt the shallows. Observation of the natural rises will soon guide you as to where they are working. As a rule, however, the fish will be found to some extent at least, between the deeps and the shallows. That area is a favourite haunt in almost all still waters and you will never go far wrong if you concentrate on where the shallow, marginal banks drop down to give way to deeper water.

If you are casting from the bank you should try to land your fly or flies (for you may have more than one wet fly on your cast if you wish) in the deeps and work it or them back into the shallows.

In the normal way you choose the side of the water from which to cast according to the wind. Naturally you prefer the wind behind you so that it helps your casting. Sometimes, however, when it is quite rough it pays to go to the other side and cast as nearly as possible into the wind, but this can be difficult and you will not be able to throw a long line. In a good wave the fish will often go quite close to the shore in the breaking water to search for the various

**43**

creatures that have been exposed from their hiding places by the turbulence.

As I have said, however, one normally goes down to the waterside from which the wind is blowing, but do not make the mistake of always trying to cast as far out as possible. Many still-water fishers invariably wade in as far as they can and then proceed to let out as much line as they can handle. In doing this such anglers will scare many fish that might have been cast over and possibly caught.

It is better to approach the water quietly and to cast along the margin before entering the water at all. Often a fish can be picked up in this way. The idea is to cover the water in front of you fanwise with a short line first. Gradually you lengthen the line covering the same arc a bit further out and so on until you have covered all the water possible without wading. After that you can go through the same procedure as you work your way out by wading. In this way you are giving yourself every chance and not wasting any water through unnecessary disturbance.

Even after you have covered all the inshore water remember occasionally to cast parallel to the shore as you wade. After you have been standing still for a time in your waders trout often work in towards where you are standing possibly because your wading has disturbed some of their food creatures from the bottom.

In the crowded conditions that are frequently experienced today on the popular reservoirs the usual procedure is to stand in one place for long spells hoping that the fish will, in their cruising, pass within your casting area. This can indeed happen, but if you are fishing a water that is not crowded it is a good idea to move along the shore as you fish. Such a movement should be very slow indeed.

Cover the whole area within reach of your casting from your first stand. Then take a slow, careful step parallel to the shore. Cover the whole of that area and then take another step—and so on. These steps must be slow and deliberate so as to cause as little disturbance and as few ripples as possible.

Reservoirs and lakes, of course, are subject to great variations of trout behaviour and the angler must use his powers of observation, see what the fish are doing and act accordingly. As a general rule I have found that usually in the morning it is a good thing to try a sunk fly—even a leaded nymph, and then to try near-surface flies during the afternoon and evening. Even if trout are to be seen rising in the early part of the day it should be remembered that at that time they usually feed on nymphs. Sometimes such nymphs are at quite a depth.

This means long casting, letting the nymph sink and then recovering it slowly. It is not a way of fishing that I particularly like, but there is no doubt that at times it may be the only way to attract the fish.

You will often find that if the fish have been taking the sunk fly or nymph during the early part of the day they may well go off it in the afternoon. Then one should try a cast of ordinary wet flies worked on the surface. Three flies on the cast is the usual number.

When nymphing one uses a long line but when surface fishing only a short line is necessary. This makes for good control of the flies and allows the angler to work the top fly along the surface—often a deadly way of attracting trout. When fishing in this way always watch carefully right up to the end of the cast because frequently a fish will follow and make its final dash at the last moment.

If you are nymphing from a boat it is sometimes better to put out an anchor which gives you time to work the long line slowly without the boat drifting down on the fly. As I have said this is probably the least interesting form of fly fishing. Much more exciting is the casting of a team of flies worked near the surface. In this way instead of only feeling the pull of a taking fish you see almost every fish that rises to the flies.

When fishing wet fly near the surface on a short line the

best procedure is to have the boat drifting across the ripple. Then you should cover the water in front of you in a fan-shaped series of casts, and if you are fishing with another angler in the boat the middle of the gunwale is your limit. Your companion then has the freedom of the other half of the water in front of the boat.

In this respect I must point out the danger of suddenly switching round to cast over a fish that has risen directly out from bow or stern. By doing this you endanger the safety of your companion. No fish is worth a hook through his ear or in his eye. In the same way a fish that rises behind the boat should be ignored. Even when fishing alone in a boat it is seldom worth bothering about fish that are seen moving out of the direct casting area. You cannot work your flies properly even if you succeed in getting over the fish and in the majority of cases it is simply a waste of time.

The angler's behaviour in a boat can be as important as the careful approach when river fishing. A boat can be a very efficient sounding board for relaying to the fish any noises made by a clumsy fisherman. One should always study to be quiet when fishing but never more so than when in a boat. Fish are extremely sensitive to noises and vibrations. Any oar movements therefore when perhaps correcting a boat's drift, should always be as gentle as possible so as to make a minimum of disturbance. Such things as knocking a pipe out on the gunwale, stamping on the floor boards or killing a fish by knocking it on seat or gunwale should never be done.

Long ago on Loch Lomond I saw a good example of how fish can react to vibrations. I had drawn the car on to a jetty which ran down to the water and noted that in the bay there were hundreds of little perch rising to flies. The water was dimpled with them giving the impression that it was raining. I was looking at this when my companion got out of the car and slammed the door. Immediately every fish over an area of about fifty yards from the jetty went down. It was ten minutes before they began to rise again.

46

In boat fishing never, on any account, stand up to cast, for not only is this bad fishing practice but it is also highly dangerous. I have seen more than one angler go head first into the water through standing to fish. It is, as I have remarked, bad fishing because the lower one can keep the better. An angler standing is visible to fish over a large area whereas when sitting down that is not so.

Another point worth remembering if you are going to do much boat fishing is always to carry a cushion of some sort as after a long day afloat the seats become very hard! Yet another comfort point to note is that sitting sideways to fish, as most of us do, can become tiring after a prolonged spell. The answer is a cross seat, which is simply a light but strong board long enough to go over each gunwale. Then the angler can sit astride such a board and fish with a straight back. Incidentally, if you are making one of these boards be sure to fit little cross pieces across each end of the board so that it will not slip inside the gunwale at any time.

When you are fishing from a boat remember that it is not any different from bank fishing in one respect—courtesy to other anglers. Never row across the drift line of another boat. Always study to go behind any other fishers so as not to upset their chances of sport. And always keep well clear of bank fishers.

Now no doubt there will be times when you are still-water fishing and the breeze falls away to leave a glassy calm on the water. This is never good for wet-fly fishing and it is often worthwhile trying a floating fly. For myself I usually put up two rods when going out on a lake or reservoir. On one I put wet flies and on the other a dry fly so that I am ready for any conditions of wind and weather which may turn up. Incidentally, if you do this be sure to stow the spare rod carefully for unless it is laid along the seats, well out of the way, it can be a nuisance.

On most waters a black fly such as a Blae and Black or a Black Spider can prove attractive to trout or if by chance there are sedges hatching out one might try a Wickham's

Fancy. I have found these three flies very good patterns for floaters on many waters in various parts of the British Isles.

Should trout be rising naturally round the boat it can make exciting fishing to cast to them and wait for their rises to your artificial. If it is calm you should cast gently so as to avoid as much as possible the making of ripples. It is almost impossible to cast without a slight ripple going out from the boat's sides but the more gently you cast the slighter will the ripples be.

In still water you will discover that a rising fish is usually travelling along as it takes down the flies. The speed at which some of these fish move will surprise you and it will pay any inexperienced angler to watch carefully one of these fish on the move. You will find that often you must cast not at the rise you have just noted but two yards or more ahead of it. Here of course you must try to guess in which direction the fish is travelling and sometimes you will be wrong because it will not always travel in a straight line. When a trout rises to your dry fly it pays, as a rule, to delay the tightening a little as compared with how you would act with the wet fly.

If fish are not rising naturally it is sometimes possible to raise the occasional one to your artificial. The idea is to cast out your fly and let it sit on the surface. Often after quite a long spell a trout will rise to it. If, however, there is no response to your sitting fly try giving it a little twitch of an inch or two along the surface and then letting it rest again. Sometimes this twitching seems to attract a passing fish to have a go at the fly. While on rivers we try to avoid drag on the fly I have seen still-water fish coming to a dry fly that was being dragged in for another cast.

When I am fishing dry fly on still water I like to use a fairly big fly—perhaps No. 12 (old size) or even No. 10. For one thing such a fly can be seen easily by the angler even in a bad light, and the bulkiness of it helps it to float properly for long periods—a most essential point.

When fishing a sedge fly in the failing light in the evening

48

one can use an even bigger pattern. Although I have always found that a fly that floats well up takes best during the day I have also found that if a sedge becomes wet through catching fish and tends to sink it will, unlike the day fly, continue to attract the trout.

Generally speaking the strike or tightening with the dry fly on still water should be rather slow, but this is purely a generalization because every rise must be treated on its merits. Sometimes fish slash at a floating fly and more or less hook themselves. Where a fish rolls at the fly, however, one should give it time to turn down again with the fly before making any attempt to set the hook.

## CHAPTER VII

# SEA TROUT

S O FAR AS fly fishing for sea trout in daylight goes the procedure is generally much the same as when fishing for brown trout. For sea trout it is usual to fish wet fly downstream and to fish dry fly upstream in the same way as for brownies.

Sea trout are shy creatures and must be approached with the greatest of caution, which is probably why the best of sea-trout fishing is to be had after dusk and into the hours of darkness. Night fishing, of course, when everything has to be done by touch, may not be everyone's idea of fun, but there is no doubt that for sea-trout fishing it is the time that is most rewarding.

If you are going to fish at night you should know the part of the river you intend to try. Should you not be familiar with the particular stretch then it is well worthwhile walking along its banks by day and studying both the river and its banks. Try to make it a rule not to wade by night. If you must wade it is absolutely essential that you know the wading conditions and even then to go particularly carefully in all circumstances.

In my experience low-water conditions are best for night work. Many times I have walked a river during the day when it was possible to see every stone on the bottom—and no fish, and have fished the same water at night to find good sport with sea trout. I have caught many sea trout at night in such conditions and I have never waded after daylight has gone. I prefer to go quietly and to cause as little water disturbance as possible even in the dark.

If you are going to night fish it is unwise to begin opera-

50

tions until the light has completely gone. This is particularly so when the water is low.

Begin at the top of your pool and work downstream very slowly. You may fish two or three flies if you wish but to avoid snags and tangles it is probably as well to use only a single fly. Every angler has his favourite patterns and it is always a good thing to use a fly in which you have confidence. For myself I have found that flies like Grouse and Claret, Butcher, Peter Ross and Wickham usually do well in almost any sea-trout water. I fish them in a fairly large size—usually No. 8 (old numbers). Let the fly come slowly round with the current, fishing it rather deep. If you have a pull that does not connect, cast over the same spot at once and possibly the fish will come again. This is a thing that does not often happen with sea trout during the day but at night they will often come a second time.

Always carry a spare cast complete and ready for use, then, if you get into a tangle or break on a snag you simply change the cast and carry on. This is much easier than trying to tie on a new fly in the dark. Incidentally you should carry an electric torch although it is not a good thing to use it indiscriminately. If you have to use the torch do not let the beam rove about over the surface of the pool but keep the light either away from the water or, if using it to net a fish keep the beam straight down.

Different rivers may vary but frequently you will find that the fish may take between darkness and midnight and then go off for a spell, beginning to take again around an hour before dawn. Once you have established the best taking times you will be able to take it easy during the off spell and begin again before the pre-dawn taking period begins. To take a break like this is better than to keep casting away for perhaps an hour or two when you have a fair idea that nothing is likely to happen.

In this night fishing you can use reasonably heavy nylon and it is a good thing to do so because it is usually in the dark hours that the big trout are likely to be hooked.

51

In still-water fishing for sea trout again much the same procedure as for brown trout can be followed. It is best done by day. I personally, have never had much success in still-water fishing after dusk. When boat fishing it is always a good thing to use a short line and work the dropper fly on the surface. There is seldom any need to cast a long line from a boat and the short line with a well-worked dropper almost always pays. One may use the usual three flies on a wet-fly cast and the size of the flies may be varied to suit the prevailing conditions. Sometimes small flies as for brown trout will do but I have almost always found that slightly bigger flies work better for sea trout. I seldom use less than No. 10s and often No. 8s for sea trout and the bigger flies seem to attract the fish more often than do the smaller ones so long as there is sufficient breeze blowing to carry them.

Sea trout, like brown trout, may be taken in the shallows and also in the deeps but as a rule I prefer to look for them where shallows meet deeps—along the edges of underwater banks or rocks. Fly patterns such a Soldier Palmer, Grouse and Claret, Peter Ross, Butcher, Dunkeld and the Pennells (either red or black) are good for still-water sea trout almost anywhere.

In the last few years dapping for sea trout has become popular and big fish are sometimes taken by anglers using this method. In dapping, a floss line and a long rod are used along with either a natural fly such as a Daddy-long-legs, or one of the many patterns of artificial dapping flies which resemble miniature flue brushes. The breeze is allowed to act on the floss line so that it billows out ahead of the boat and so that the single fly used is tripping along the surface of the water. Hooking fish that rise to the dap can be difficult until the angler has had some experience. One must be slow and to tighten too soon simply pulls the fly clear of the fish. Many anglers find this a fascinating way of fishing but for myself I prefer to fish the normal wet fly in the good old-fashioned way. It is of course a matter of personal choice. To a beginner I would give the advice to have a trial of each method of fly fishing and then to try to perfect the method that appeals most to him.

## CHAPTER VIII

# SALMON

HAVING FISHED FOR trout with the fly there should be little difficulty in trying for salmon with the fly. The main difference is that your tackle is generally heavier so far as salmon are concerned. There is no need to fish very light for salmon at any time and one should always be sure that the tackle is capable of standing the strains of playing the bigger fish. Generally, the weight of nylon for the cast is governed by the size of the fly being used; where a big fly is in use nylon up to perhaps 20 lb. breaking strain may be required. On the other hand if one is fishing very small, low-water flies in summer when levels are low the nylon may be reduced to perhaps 8 or 10 lb. breaking strain. I would never advise anything less than such breaking strains for salmon at any time.

Heavy nylon never kept a salmon from taking yet, but light nylon has often been broken by heavy fish, letting them go free with a hook in their mouths and trailing a length of nylon behind them. Trout may respond to light nylon as against heavy but salmon never do and it is not good fishing to risk breakage unnecessarily.

The usual procedure when fly fishing for river salmon is to start at the top of a pool and work slowly down it. Some people fish down fairly quickly and then repeat the process before going on to the next pool. My own preference is for very slow fishing when salmon are concerned and if I am on a pool that I like I am quite happy fishing it for hours on end. I fish down slowly and then, keeping well back from the water, return to the top and go down again.

Salmon are not easily scared, as are trout, by the passing of a human on the bank but it does no harm to pretend that they are. Always therefore keep well back from the water when walking by a pool you intend to fish. This should be rigidly observed when another rod is fishing the pool.

Always fish the fly slowly across the current where salmon are concerned and in spring or autumn do not be afraid to let your fly be well sunk.

In summer when fishing the greased line method I still prefer my fly to be some four inches under the surface. For this reason I do not fish a floating line but instead I grease an ordinary line leaving about five yards ungreased at the end. This end piece goes under and ensures that the fly is below the surface and unable to skate.

When a fish does rise to your fly the main thing to keep in mind is to avoid any hurry in tightening on it; slowness is very important if one is to hook salmon properly. From the way in which salmon come to a near-surface fly you may see your fish before it has taken the fly in its mouth and striking on sight therefore will simply drag the fly away from the fish. Each rise should be judged on its merits but in nine cases out of ten the pattern is the same.

The fish follows the fly across the river and then it surges ahead to take, usually across the line of the fly's travel. Having taken the fly the fish then comes on turning downstream and so round again to return to its lie. If you see the fish at all it is only during the actual taking surge. The rest of the movement is under the water. Proof that the fish has carried on and turned downstream after taking can be had from noting the side of the mouth in which the hook has fastened. You may hook a fish and swear you are sure that it is hooked in say, the right side when on examination you find that it is hooked in the left. For example, if you are fishing down a pool with your right side towards the water and a fish follows the fly, rises and is hooked you might imagine that it was hooked in the right of its jaw since that was the side nearest to you as you fished. However, in most cases, if the strike has been properly delayed, you will find that the hook is in the left jaw. The hook has been pulled to that side through the fish having turned towards you and downstream after its taking surge.

Some people advise a loop of line to be hanging from the reel and let go when a fish takes. Long ago I tried this and when the first fish I hooked whipped the loop out, part of that loop went round the reel. After that I decided the loop idea was not a good one.

The safest way I found to give slack to a taking fish is to keep your rod point fairly high as you fish. In a fast stream you may have to hold it very high to give a slack belly of line between rod point and water and when a fish takes you can give more slack by dropping the rod point. Another way of giving slack is to fish with your reel on a very light check and simply let the salmon pull line off after it takes. The reel adjustment can then be tightened to play the fish.

When playing a salmon you must not be rough on it but you must always be firm. Remember that the rod is intended to take the strain and it should be kept well bent against the fish. Those who take a very long time to play a salmon are in danger of losing it, for as time goes on the hookhold wears and thereafter the least slackening of the line may allow the barb to slip out.

Landing a salmon may be done by gaffing, netting, tailing or beaching. To gaff I like to put the gaff hook over and below the fish; a smart draw upwards will then impale the fish and it can be lifted quite slowly to the shore. Never jerk the gaff home and carry on the stroke violently or you may throw the fish off the gaff. Your movements must be firm but controlled. In netting a salmon pretend (as I told you in the case of a big trout) you are netting only the middle cut. That is to say if the fish is longer than the diameter of the net the head must be led over and past the net ring before the net is lifted. If you do this quite a big fish will curve upwards nicely and slip into the meshes, but if you lift before the head is far enough over the fish will simply slide back into the water. For tailing, your fish must be played out and

*Gaffing a salmon*

floating. Grip it firmly by the wrist of its tail and you will find that your grip will not slip nor will the fish struggle once you have lifted it.

Beaching is I think, the best way of landing a salmon and it can be done on even a very small beach or inlet on the river bank. The procedure is much the same as for trout— but more care must be taken with the heavier fish. The ideal places, of course, are where sand or shingle slope gently into the water. The fish should be brought in while there is still some life in it, unlike the other methods of landing in which the fish should be completely played out. With still a few yards of line out the angler, holding the line against the rod with his hand, should walk slowly back-

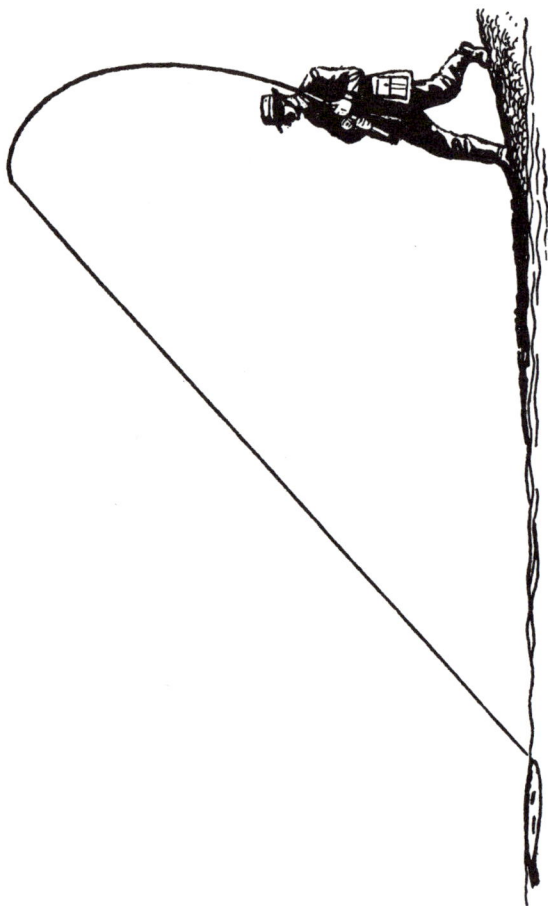

*Beaching a salmon*

wards keeping a steady pressure on the rod. When the fish begins to leave the water it will give the occasional kick, and with each kick it will help to push itself up the beach. When the fish is clear of the water it may then be picked up by the wrist of the tail. Again there must be no hurried movements—everything should be done slowly and methodically. It will be found that once the fish is up on the beach and the rod pressure relaxed, the fish will lie still.

If salmon are to be kept they should be killed at once by a sharp blow between the eyes. In spring, of course, kelt fish will be caught and these must, by law, be returned to the water. Gaffs naturally must not be used on such fish. In autumn too, salmon that are heavy in spawn should be handled gently and returned.

In boat fly fishing for salmon on still water one uses a short line as in boat fishing for trout. For salmon two flies are normally used—one on the tail of the cast and one near the top of the cast as a dropper. This dropper can be a deadly fly if it is worked carefully across the water surface when it is being retrieved. Always work the flies right in to the shadow of the boat because salmon have a habit of following right in and taking at the last moment. They do not, incidentally, seem to be scared of boats or oars to any great extent.

Where trout or sea trout are concerned the first rod to fish down a pool or to cover a still-water drift may have the best chances of catching fish. Where salmon are concerned, however, this does not hold. The last man over the fish will have as much chance of success as the first so long as those who have gone before are fishing normally and have made no particularly bad disturbances.

In still-water fishing it is very important to delay the strike when a fish rises. Normally you will see the salmon right in front of you as it rolls over, but if you strike on sight you will simply pull the fly away from the fish. Wait till the fish has gone out of sight before you tighten. If you are in any doubt as to whether or not the fish has taken you should watch the line and do nothing until it moves. If by chance the fish misses the fly simply let the fly sit still and sometimes the fish will take a turn under water before coming back and gripping the sinking fly firmly.

If you are fishing for salmon, say in a Highland loch, you will find that the best taking places are comparatively shallow—often where shallows slope down to meet the deeps. You may see fish plunging in the deeps but it is wise to pay little attention to them as they are probably travelling fish which would not take anyway.

Always have plenty of backing on your reel when still-water fishing for salmon. Often these fish make long runs and if by chance you foul hook one of them it is sure to make the line fly.

## CHAPTER IX

# TAILPIECE

IT WOULD NOT be right to finish a book for beginners without drawing their attention to the importance of good behaviour when fishing.

In the old days anglers were noted for their good sporting manners. Nowadays, however, with great numbers of newcomers on the waterside every season there are too many who do not realize that a most important point in fishing is thoughtfulness for the other fellow.

The beginner should always have in mind that good manners are an essential part of fishing. Even if you do nothing to upset the fish and so spoil another's chances, try not to do anything that might upset another angler. Fishing is a quiet and (should be) a pleasant sport. If a man is annoyed by anything while he fishes it may tend to spoil his day.

If you go down to the river to fish and find an angler already fishing there you do not on any account start to fish anywhere near him and certainly never in front of him. You may start behind him but if you particularly want to fish the same pool that he is on you should wait until he has finished it. This may be subject to some variation on very big pools or where salmon fishing on a big river is concerned, but if in any doubt don't risk doing the wrong thing.

Never be afraid to ask another angler where you may start so as not to interfere with his sport. Tell him you are a beginner and he will almost certainly do what he can to help you and to guide you. Again, however, never approach a man to talk to him while he is actually fishing. If you wish to speak to him be sure to wait until you see that he has paused to change a fly or to do something of the sort, and if you approach the water see that you do so carefully so as not to disturb the part he is likely to fish. When you have finished speaking withdraw as carefully as you approached until you are well out of the range of his back cast.

Should a man be fishing under a high bank it is always a bad move to go forward and speak to him from that bank. In so doing you are disturbing all the fish in the area and he, crouching below to keep out of sight, will certainly not be pleased.

If at all possible avoid wading. If wade you must be sure that you are not ruining the chances of any angler who may be following you. Much trouble, especially on smaller rivers, has been caused by unnecessary wading. In some cases indeed, the outcome has been a banning of wading altogether.

Generally in the country places one should study not to be noisy. If by chance you happen to be of the mentality that needs to take a transistor radio with it on a fishing trip you may well expect to find it—and yourself—suddenly under water.

Gates should be left as found and, of course, no litter should ever be left lying. Always see that your car is left in a place where it will not obstruct other traffic. Even in a country lane a farmer may want to enter the gateway you have chosen as your parking place, and that farmer may well be the owner of the fishing rights too!

When boat fishing never cross another boat's drift unless you are a good distance from that boat. Should you be rowing from one bit of the water to another be sure to go behind any boat you may be near on your way. If you are using an engine you must be doubly careful of your movements so as not to create disturbance to others. Never stand up in a boat to fish. When in boats you should go quietly as possible with as little thumping of feet on floorboards or splashing of oars as possible and remember that water carries vibrations and vibrations are warning sounds to fish.

Now all these do's, dont's and never's really boil down to

good manners and thought for the other fellow. I may have repeated some items I mentioned earlier. If I have done this it is because I consider such items important. If we can keep our good manners up to a high pitch it can be all the better, it can make more pleasant and more productive fishing for all of us. Equally important, it can save those waterside rows which blow up from time to time and which are completely foreign to the quiet sport.

In the good behaviour direction there is an item to which I must draw special attention. It is to plead with every angler never to leave unwanted nylon lengths lying about either in the water or out of it. Terrible things have happened to birds and animals through their becoming entangled with nylon. I have known of countless cases of legs and wings being cut to the bone and of lingering deaths of many creatures having been caused in this way. Even sheep have had to have legs amputated because of damage through nylon entanglement. Only recently I heard of a trout entangled in nylon and cut right through to the backbone with it.

I am quite sure that no angler wants to cause suffering or death to any living thing through his carelessness, yet every season the list of casualties mounts up. I ask you therefore, to exercise constant care in this direction and also to miss no opportunity of passing on word to fellow anglers of the sad consequences of leaving nylon lying about.

If you have some unwanted nylon you can roll it up and cut it into small pieces with your scissors before throwing it away, or you can put a match to the roll and see that it is burnt down to short pieces. Best of all is to put it in your bag or pocket and burn the lot when you arrive home.

\*     \*     \*

With that I come to the end of this little book. I hope it has helped you to make a successful start with fly fishing.

As you progress you will find that experience is the best teacher of all. Be observant and thoughtful as you fish and success will surely follow.

## THE END